the COLORING BOOK for the SUPER INTELLIGENT

ISBN-13: 978-0961535605
LCCN: 2014911900

PHILADELPHIA
PENNSYLVANIA

Together
we can color
our worlds
to make our
dreams
come true.

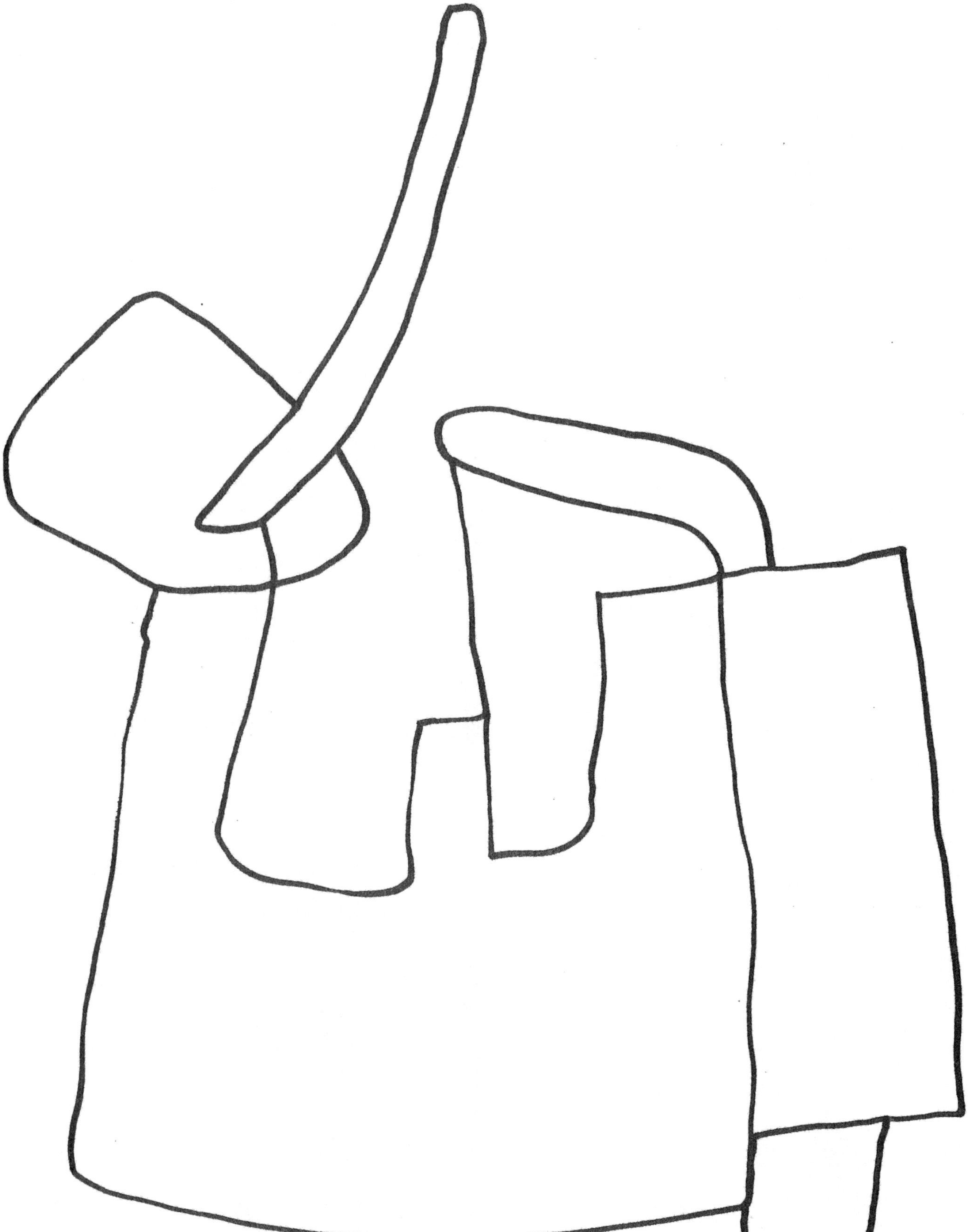

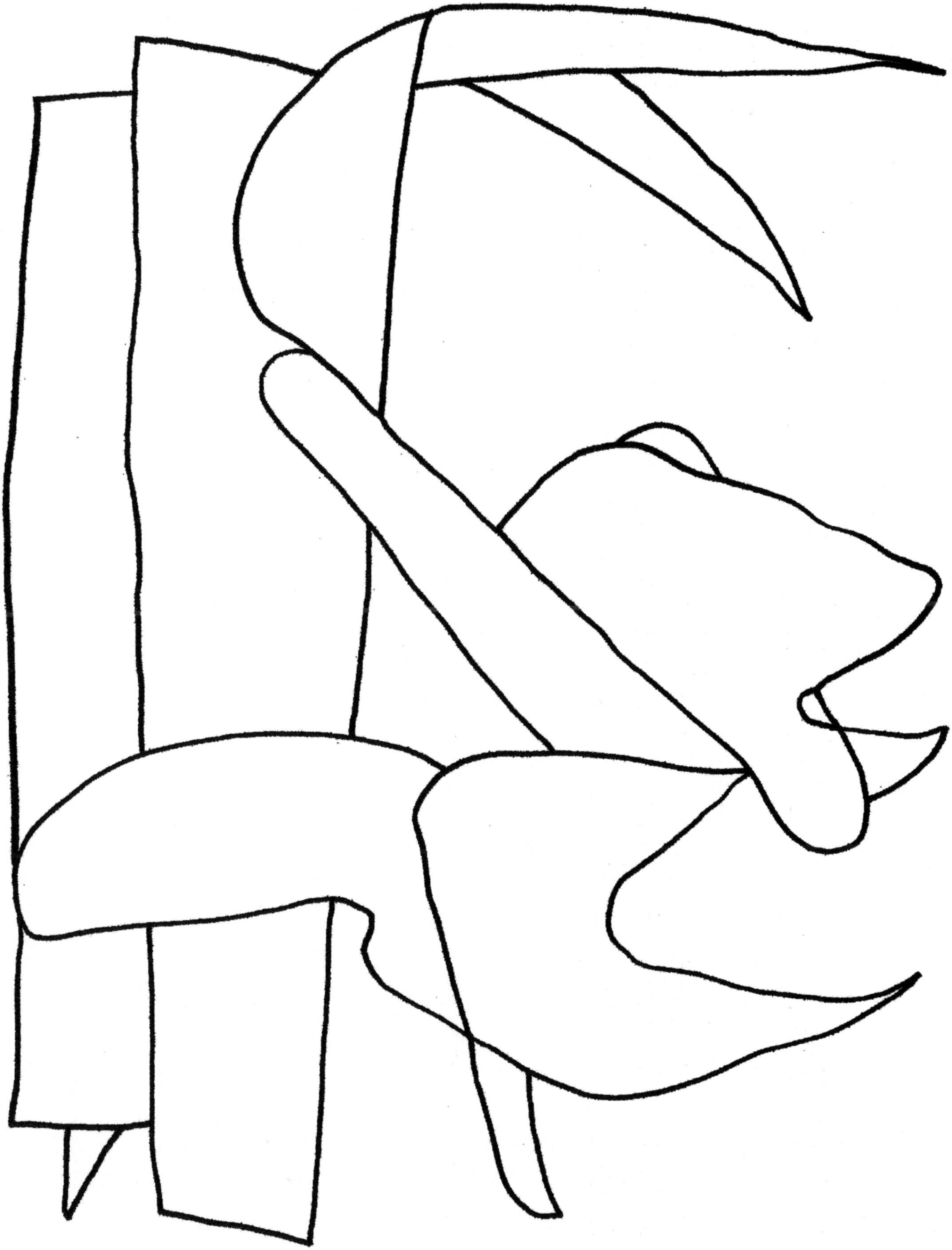

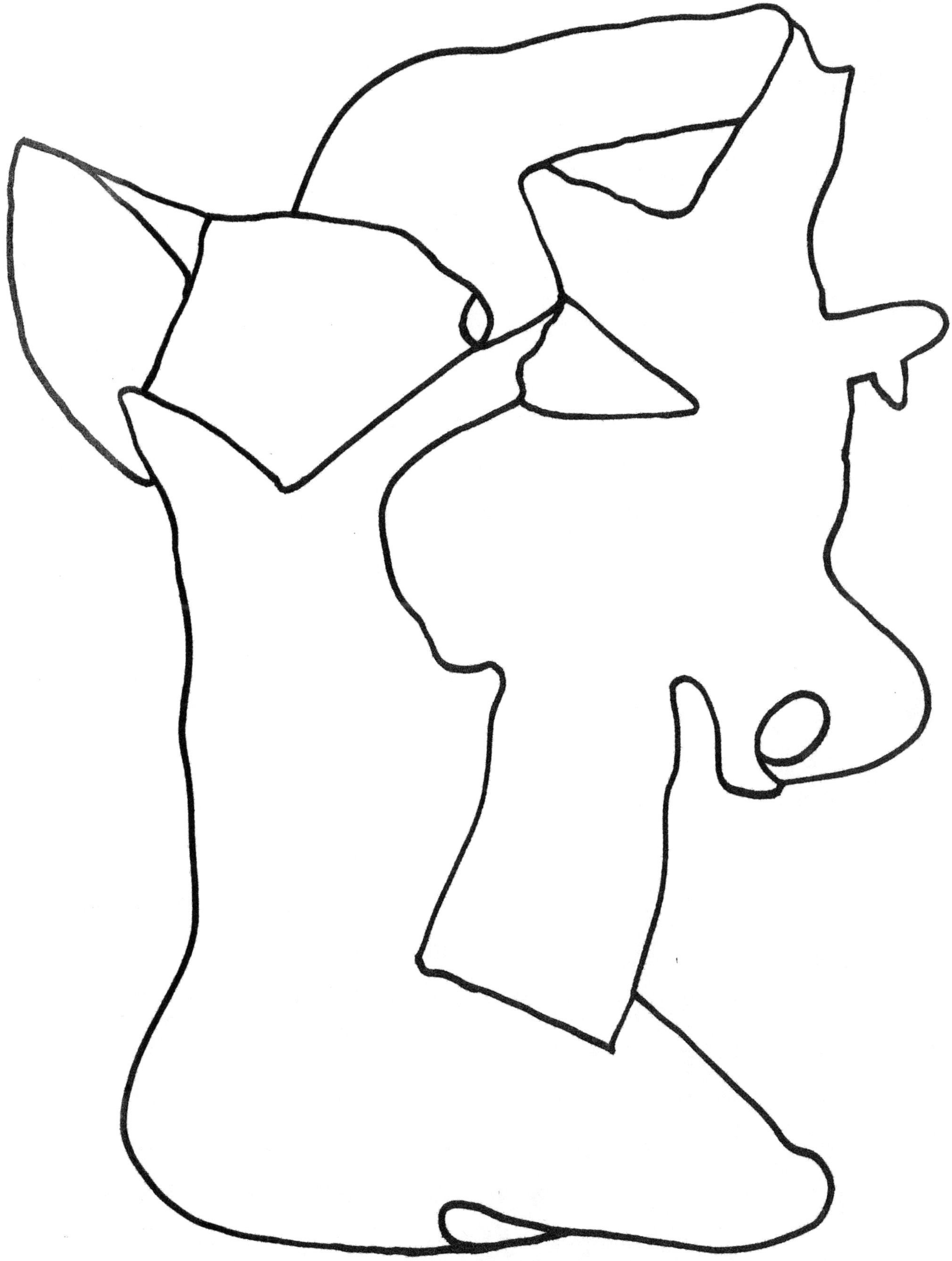

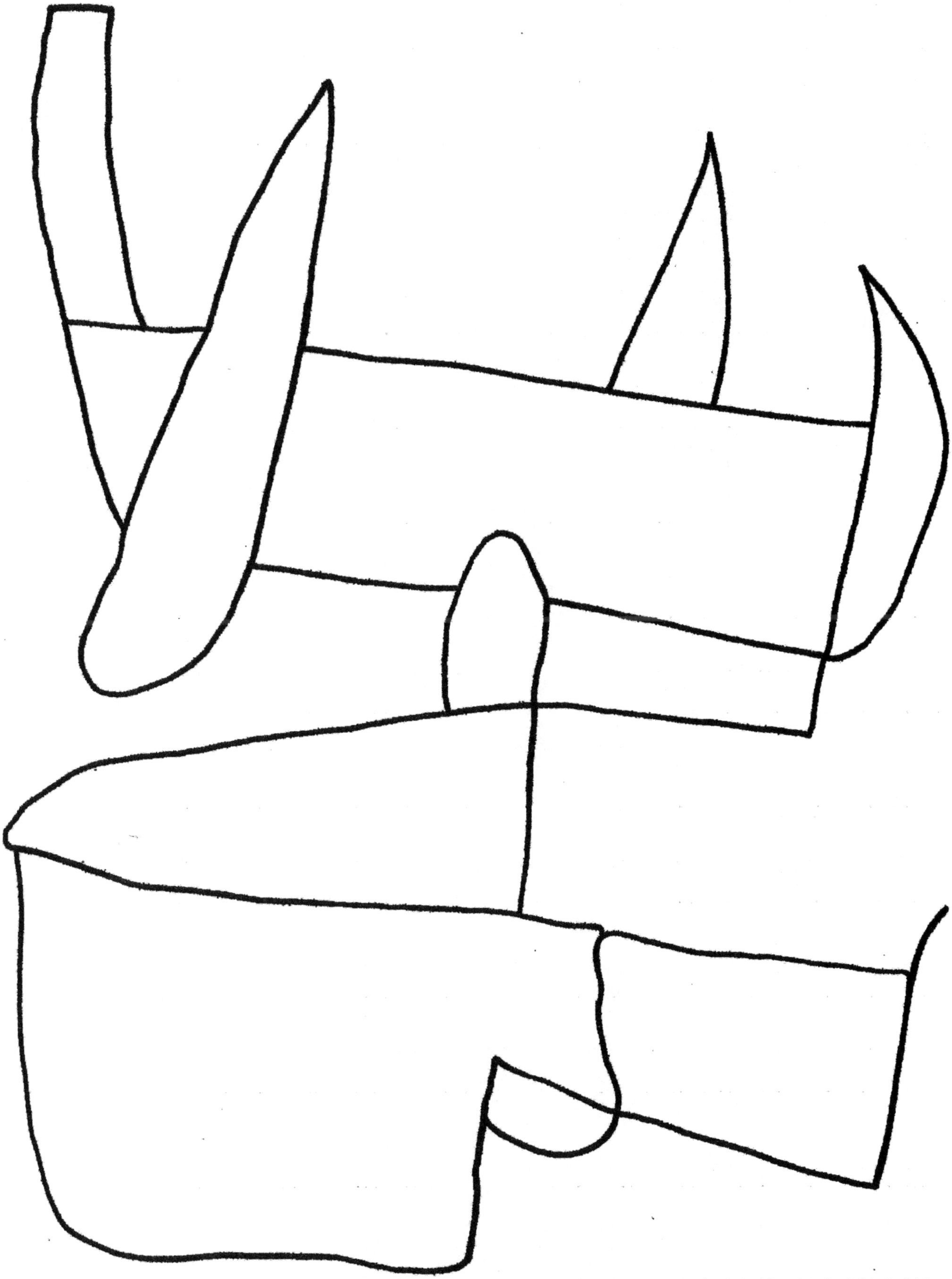

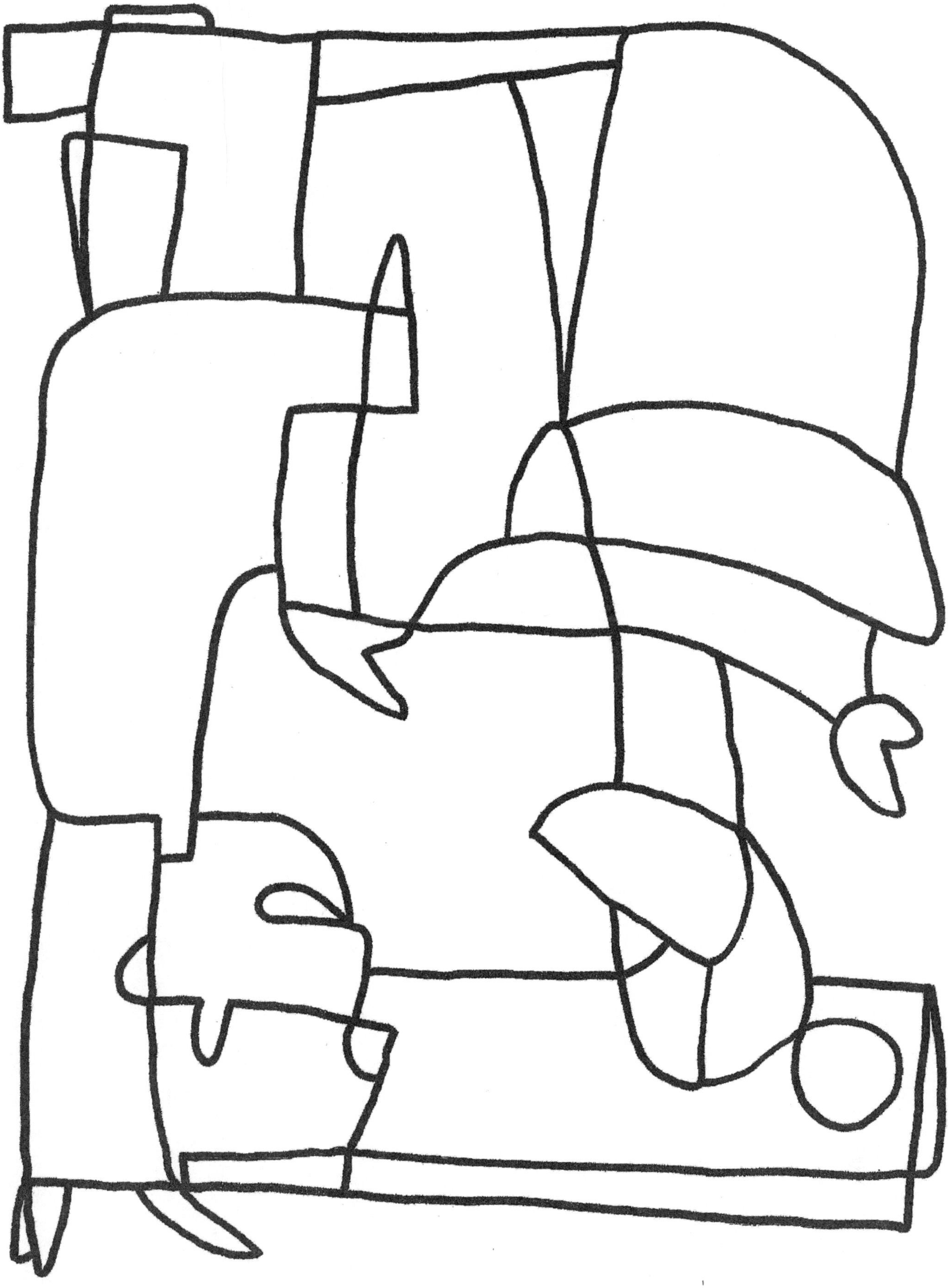

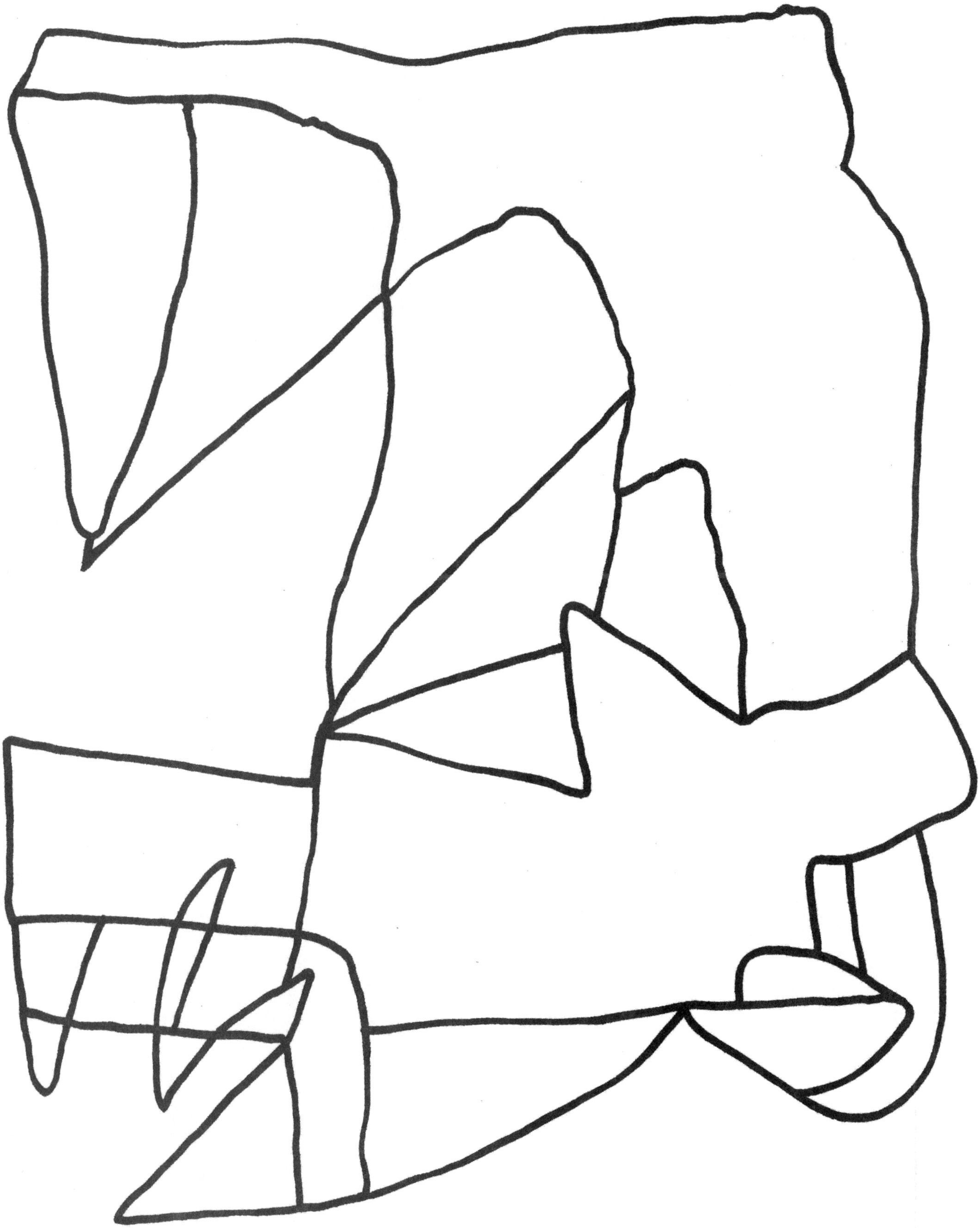

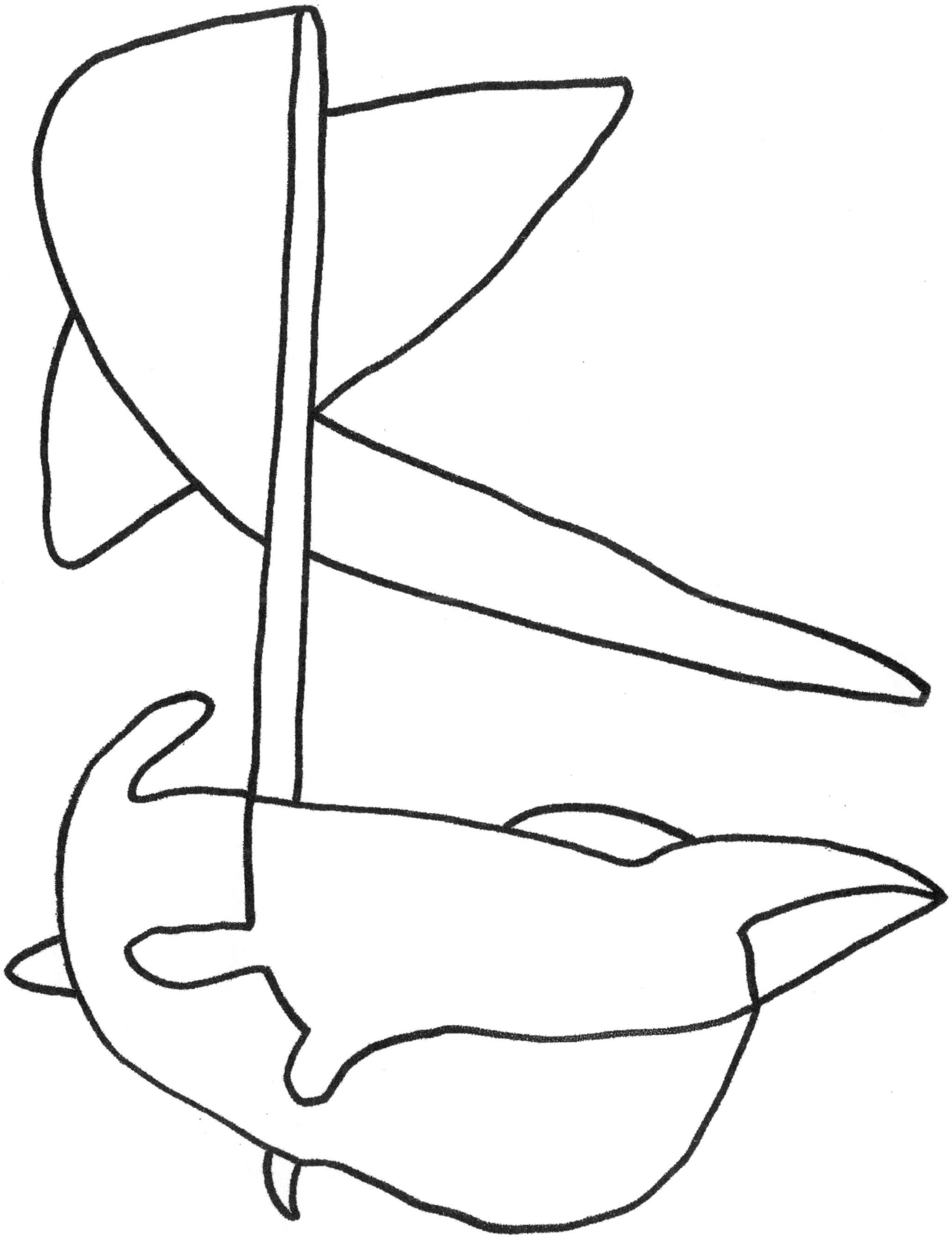

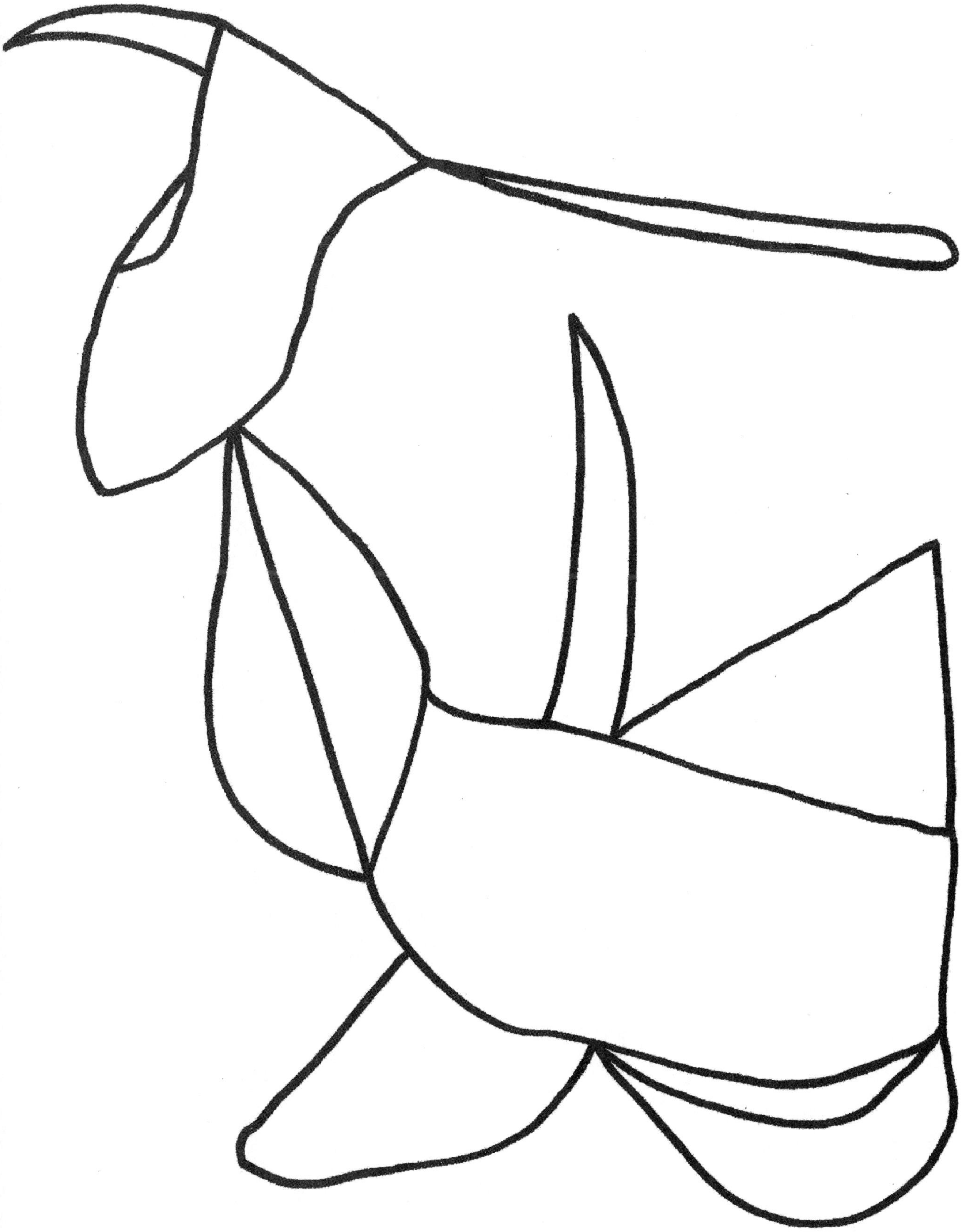

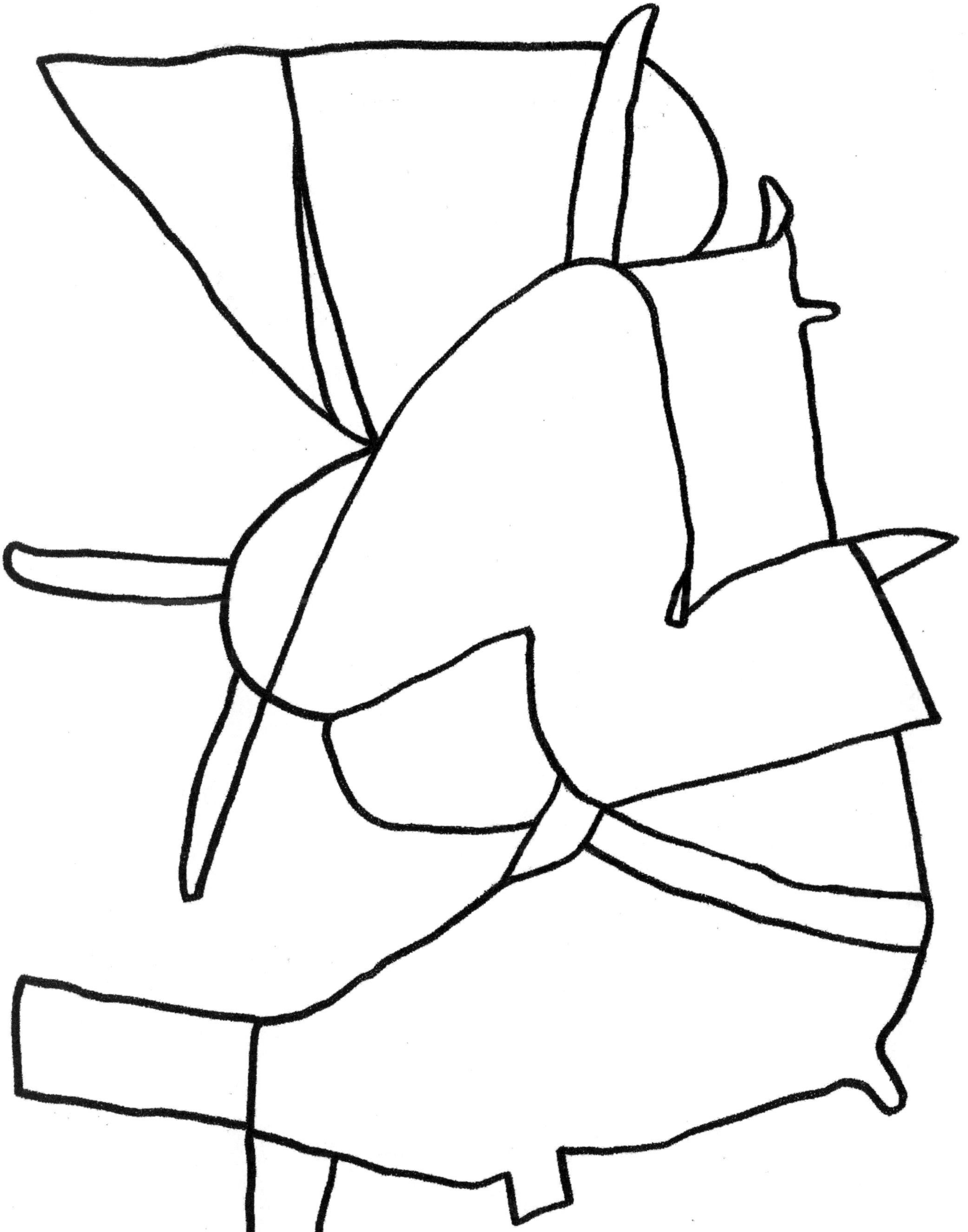

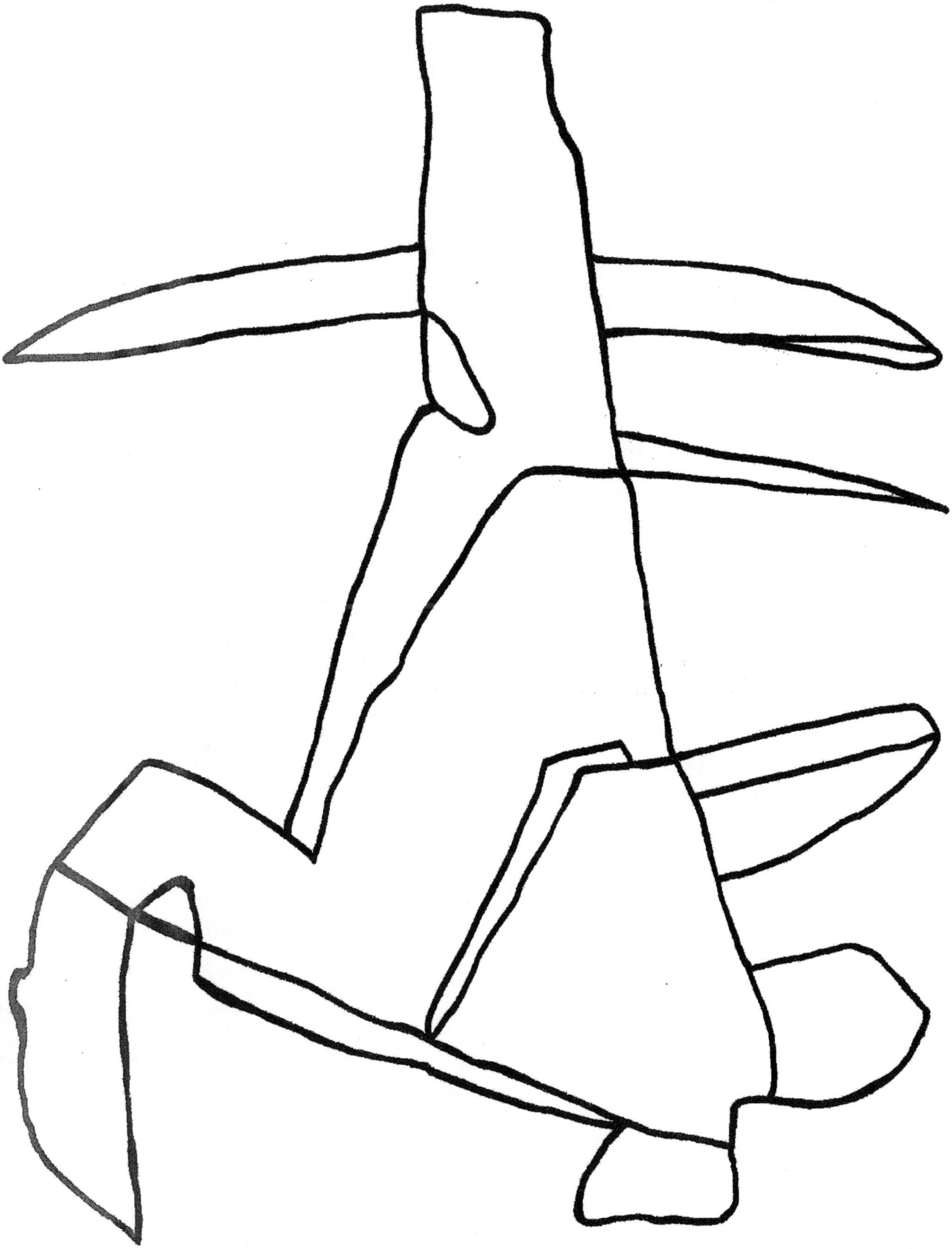

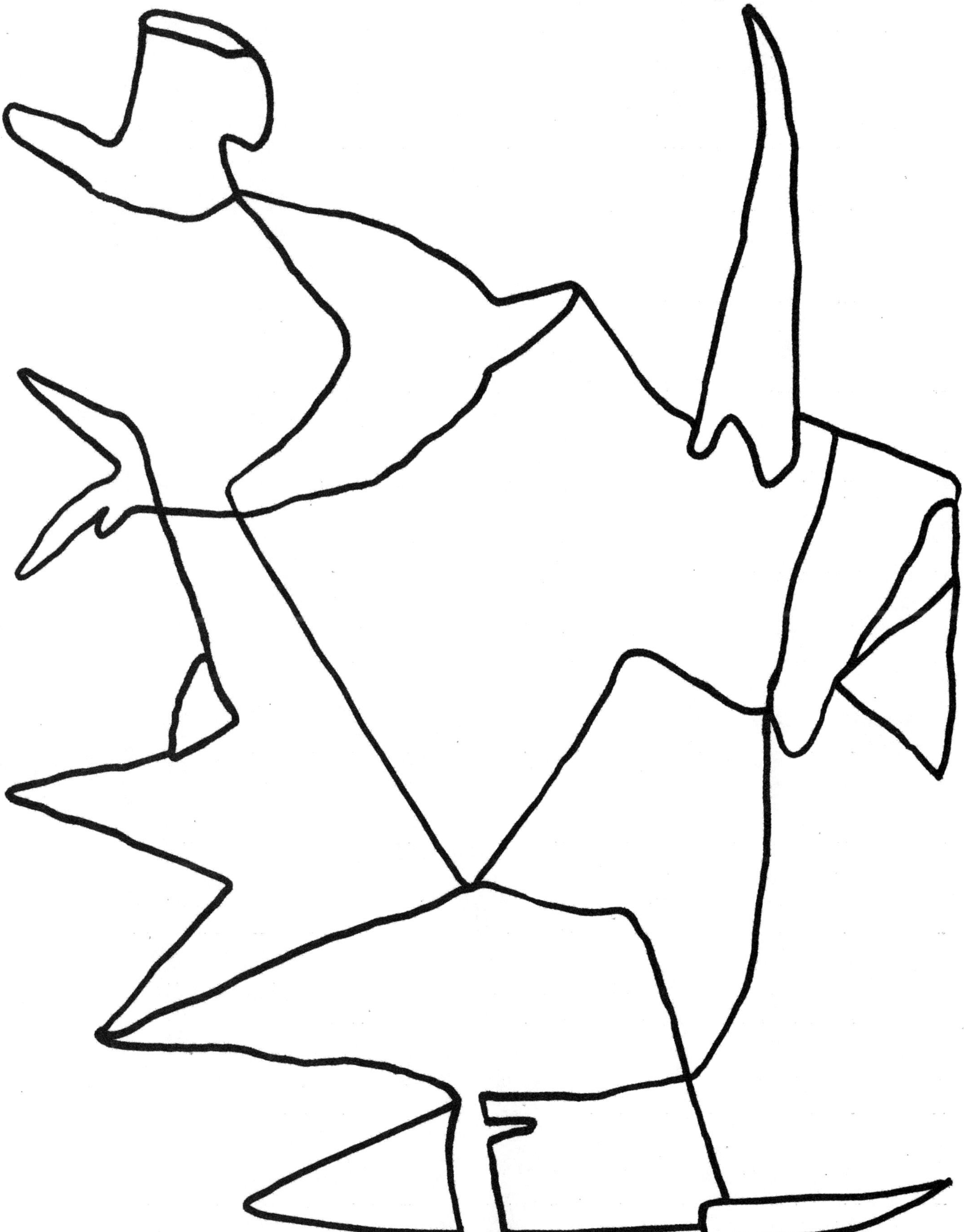

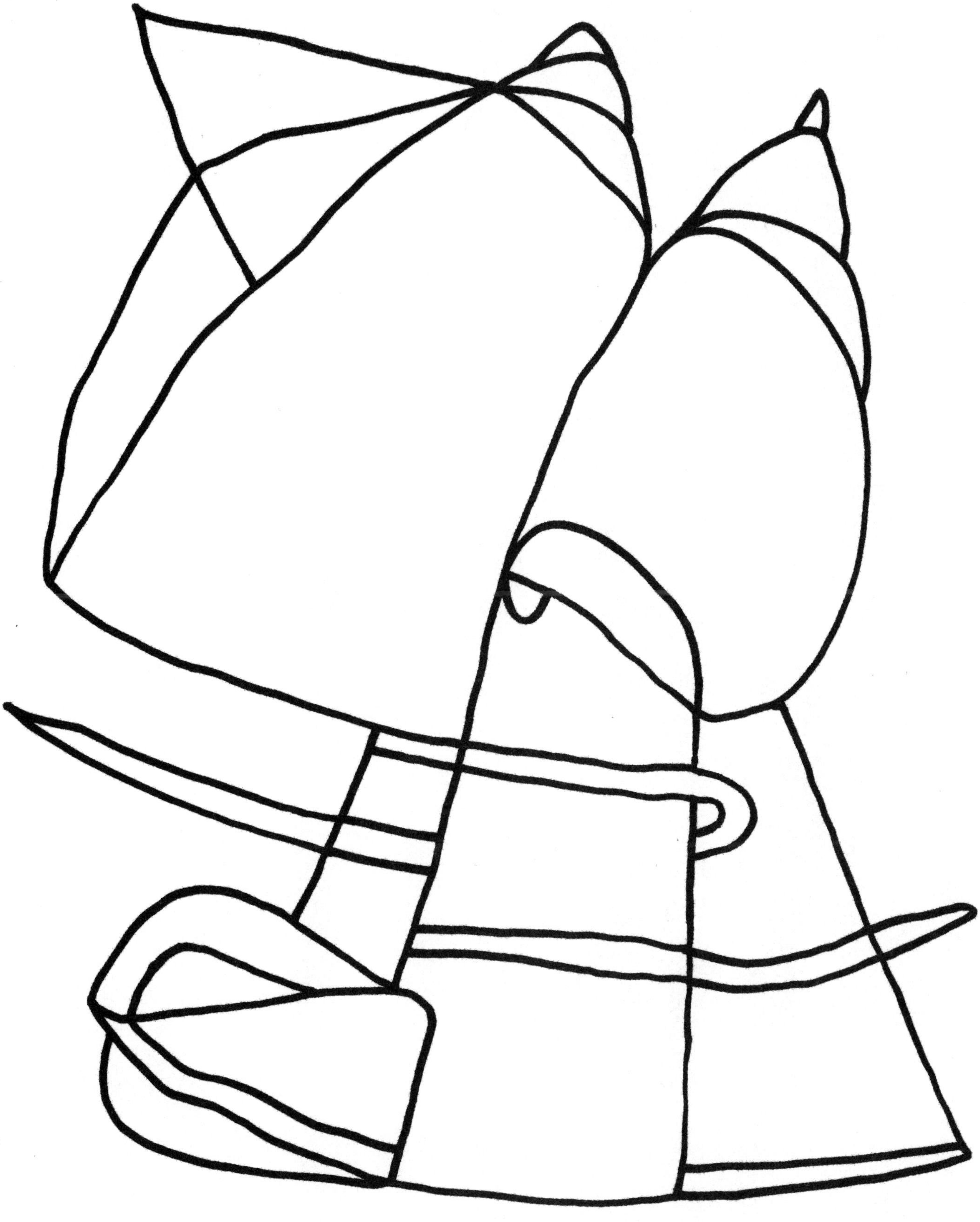

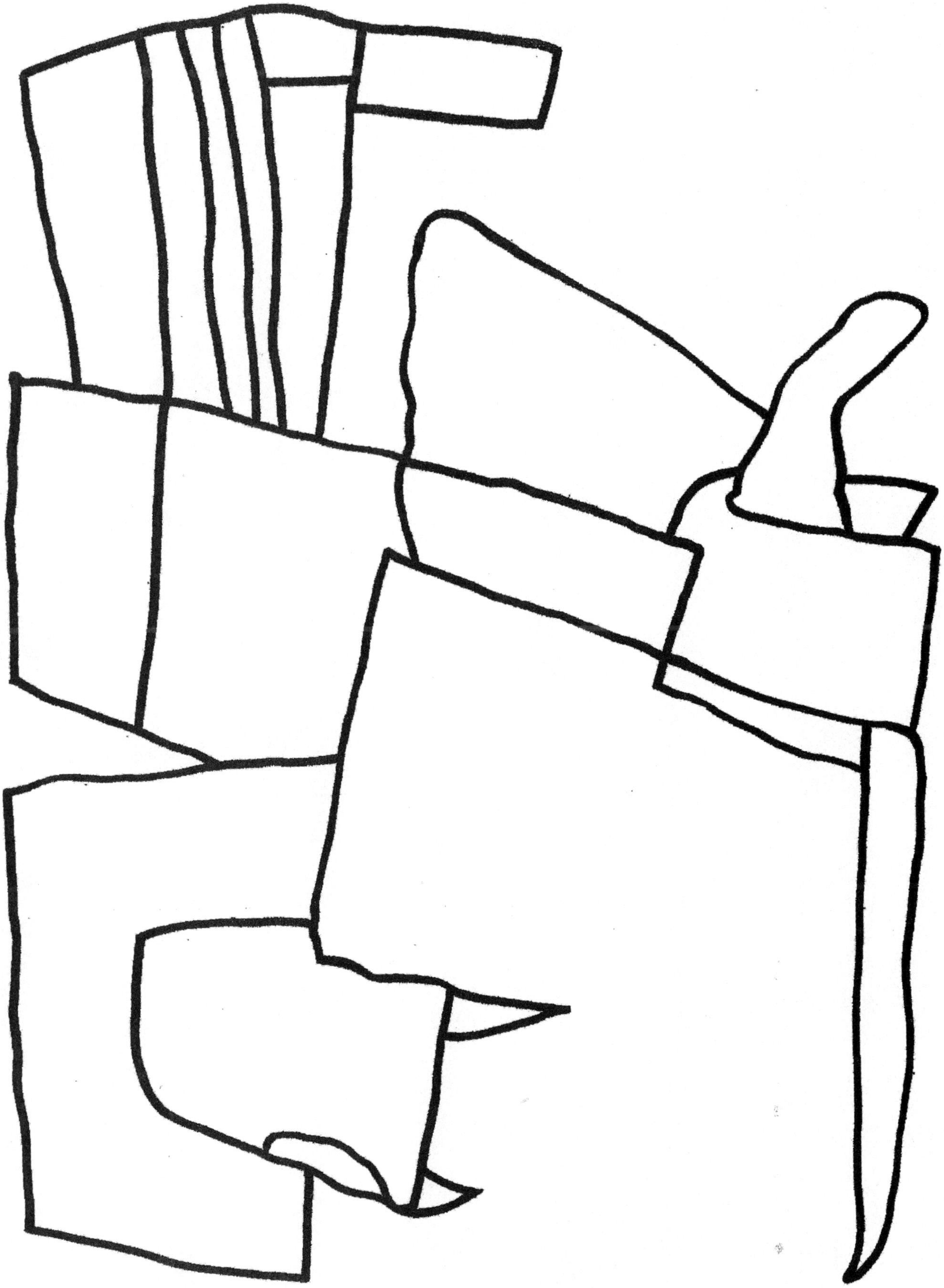

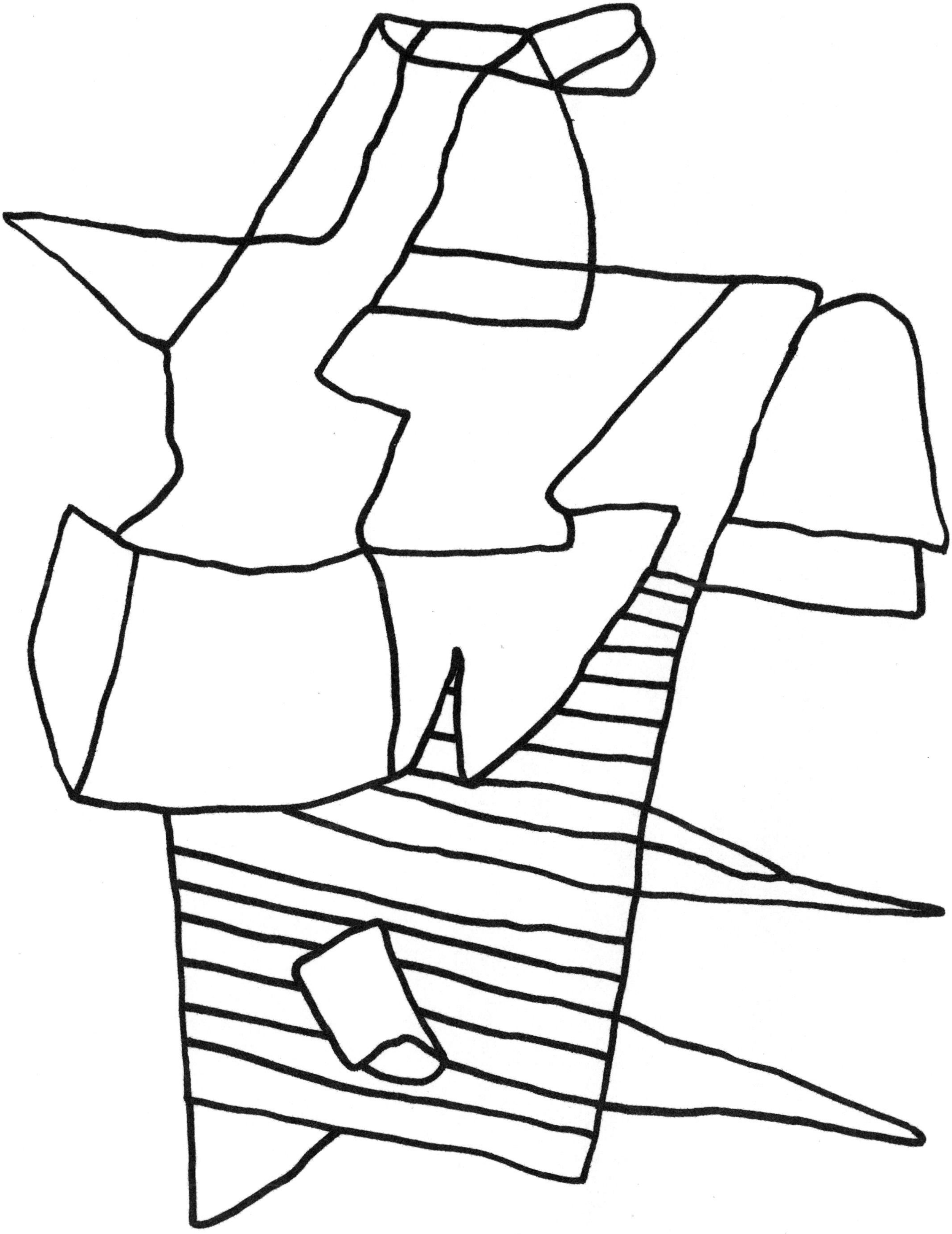

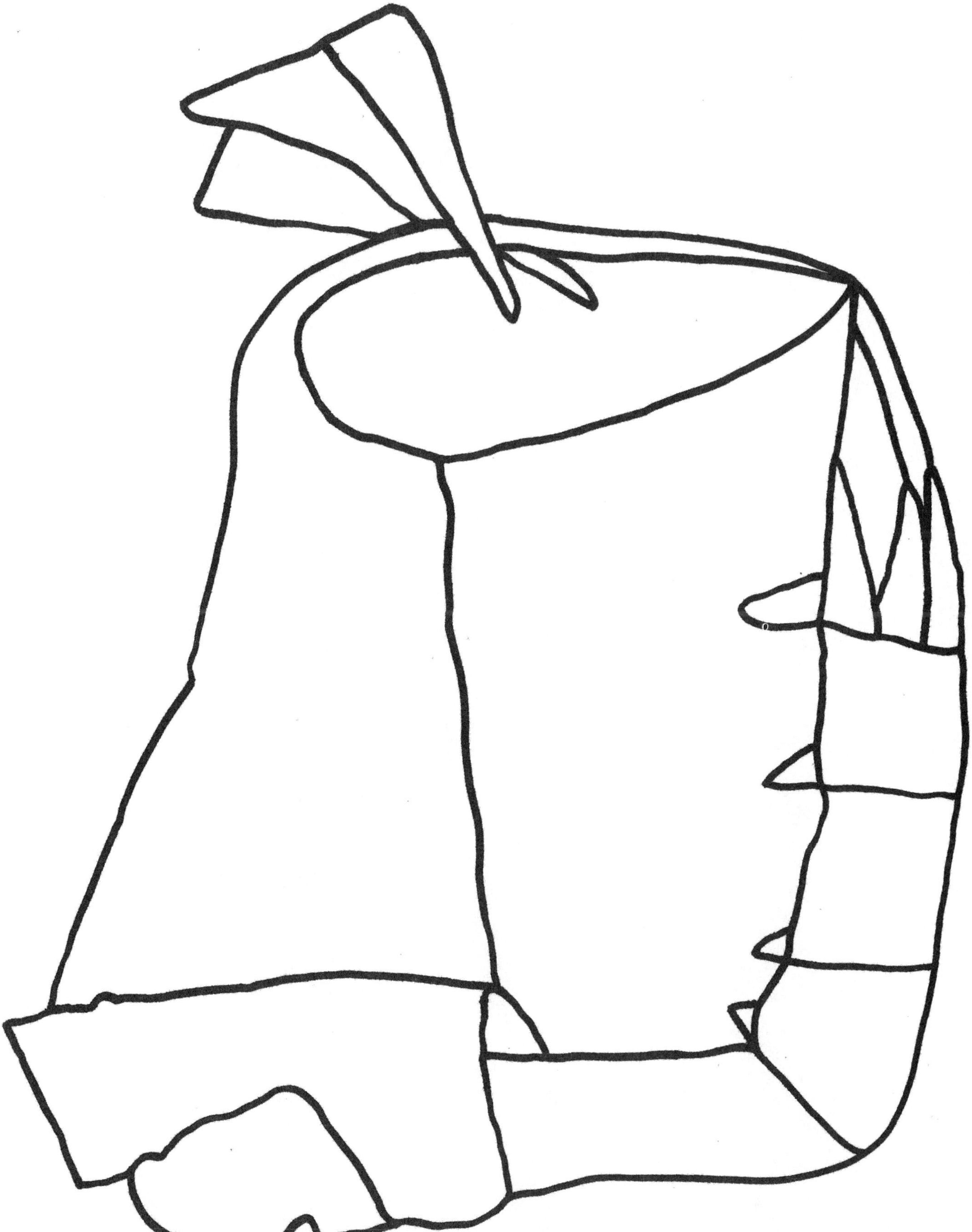

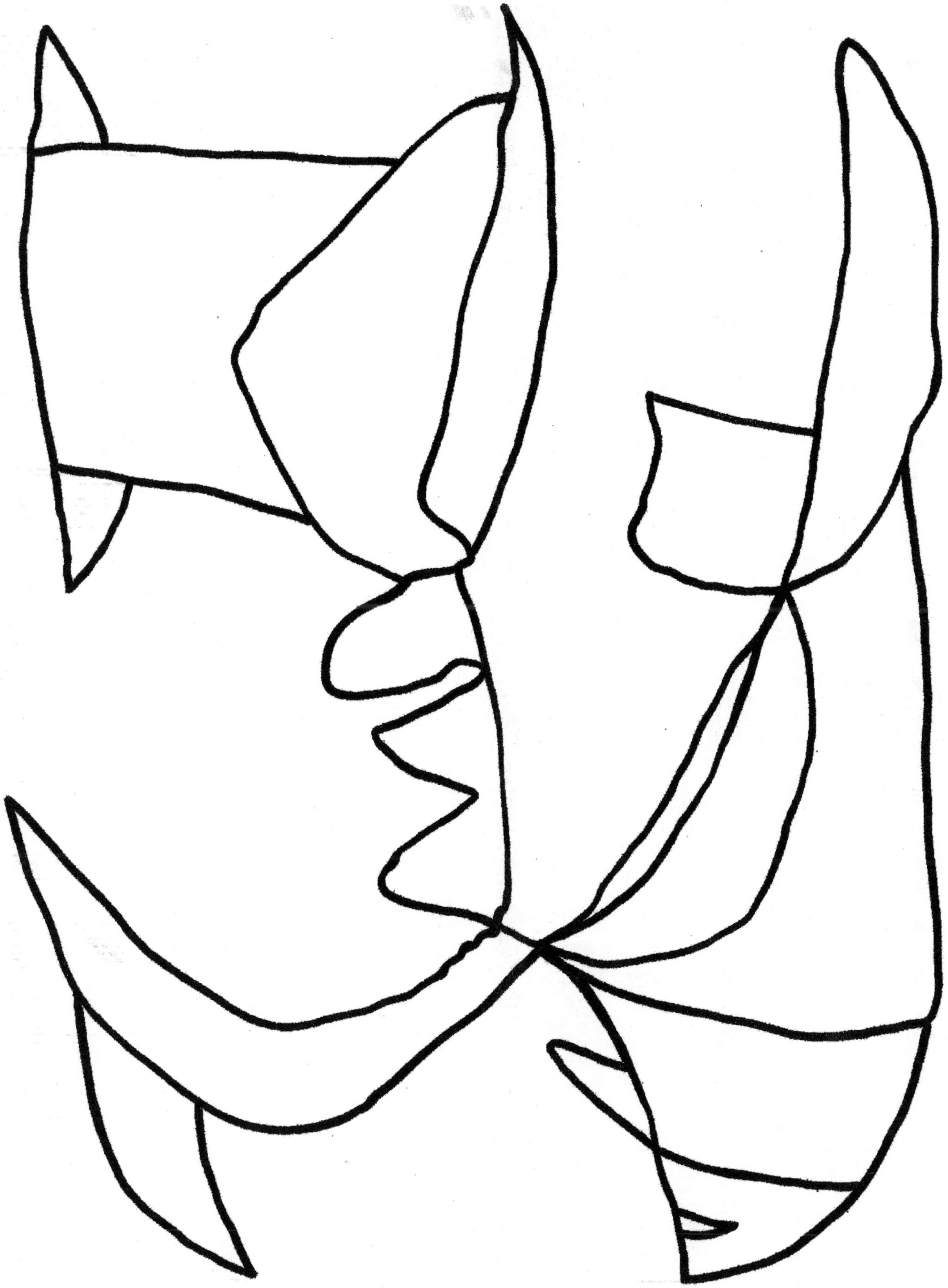

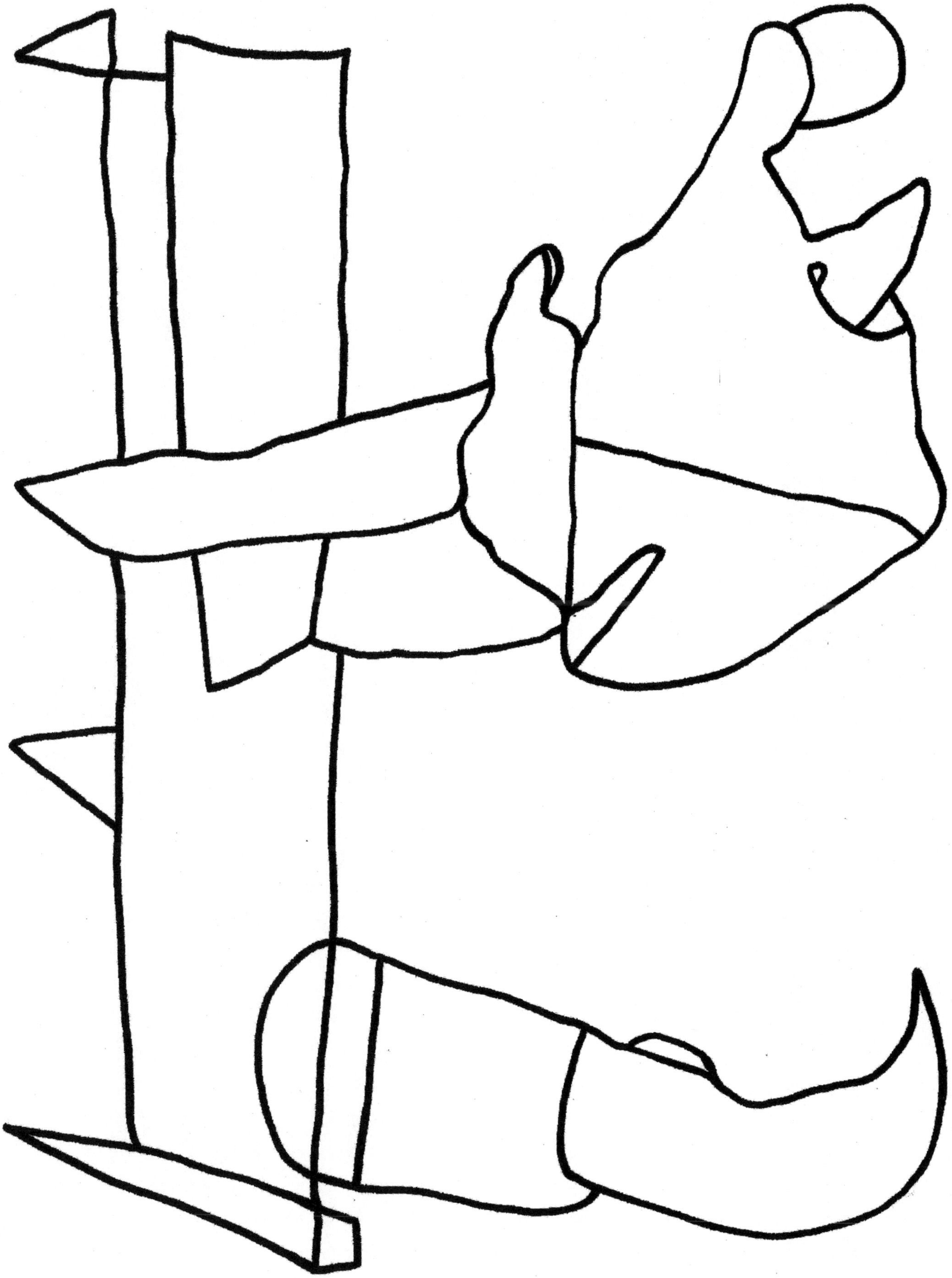

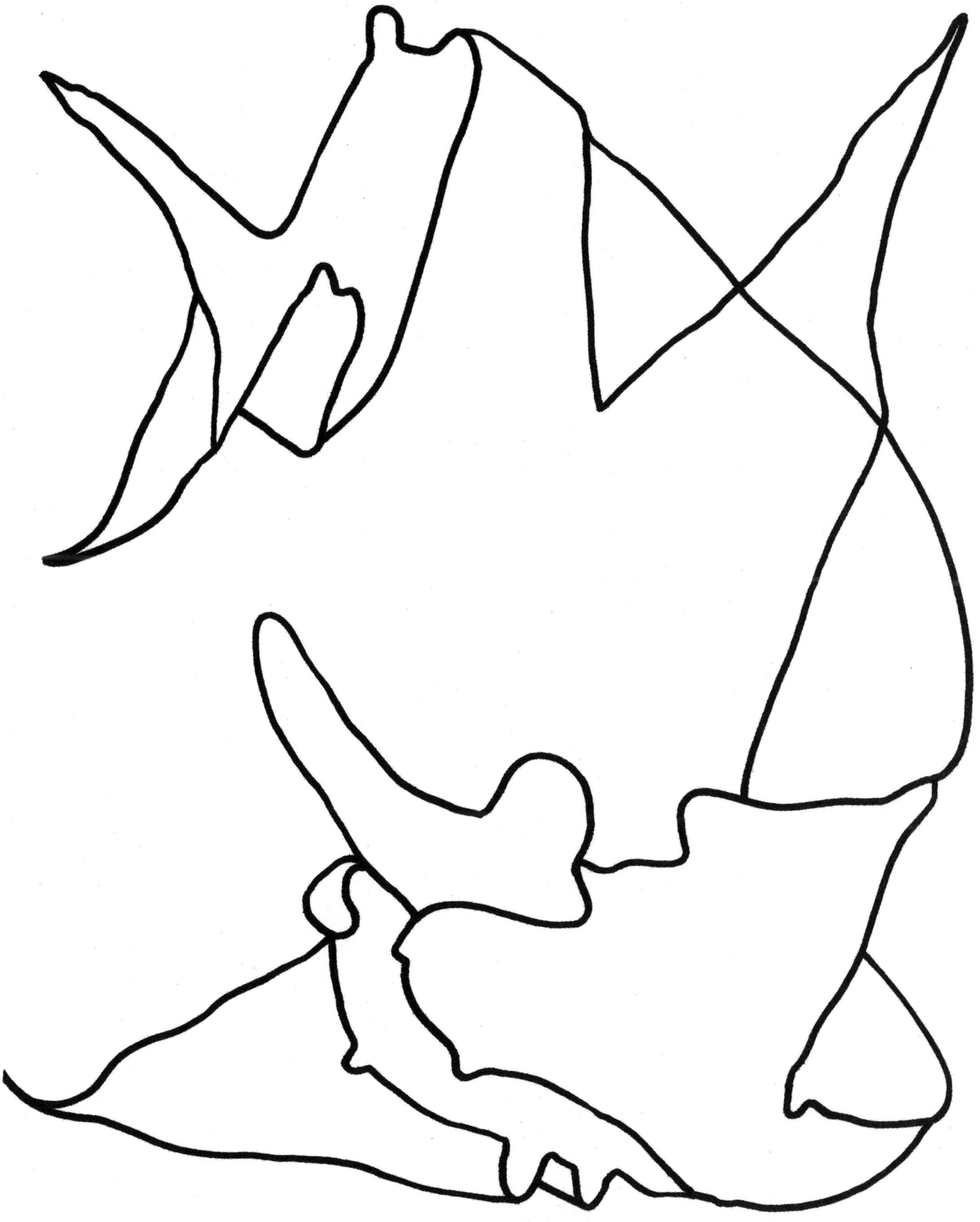